AF507365

# Glimpses of Heaven

A Very Small Book™
by Bob Higgins

Published by Sure Marketing
365 NE Greenwood Ave #3
Bend, OR 97701 | https://sure.marketing

Sure Marketing maximizes the reach of churches and nonprofits, specializing in online promotion of Christian ministries.

First printing November 2022
Second printing April 2023
Third printing October 2024

Printed Worldwide

ISBN 979-8-218-49020-1 (paperback)

For more of Bob's writing, visit his blog at:
medium.com/@robertjhiggins

Cover Photography by agsandrew on Adobe Stock
Cover & Interior Design by Brent Earwicker

*Dedicated to Carol, my wife of 54 years,
who now enjoys the glories of heaven.*

# Contents

# Preface

**My Wife, Carol, died in October, 2020.**

That centered a lot of my thinking on Heaven. Since she was a fresh arrival there, I pondered how she was fitting into her new surroundings. What was she experiencing as the first sights, the first introductions, the first encounters with saints, angels, and God Himself unfolded?

This Very Small Book™ is the result of my wondering how Carol was doing as a new resident in Heaven.

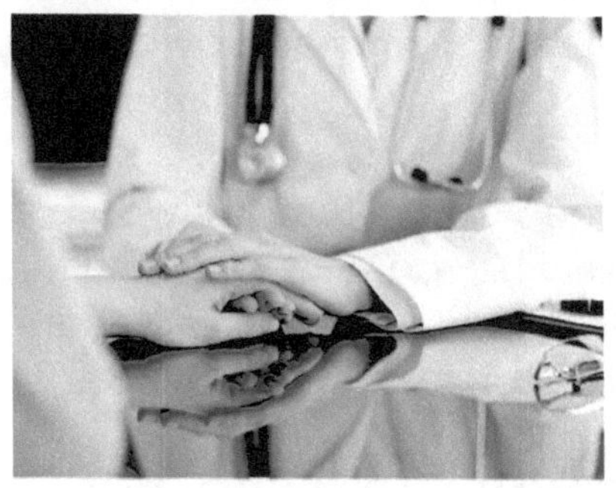

# **Chapter 1: No Anxiety**

*When faced with certain death, how can we be at peace?*

**I have asked myself the question, "How could Carol have had no anxiety at all when the doctor announced, 'You have days or weeks to live'?!"**

It was final. There was no doubt he was right. He had done all he could do with every medical treatment at his disposal. Many years of experience left him with no other option than to declare, "days or weeks." The spinal tap confirmed his dreaded suspicions: He had no more help to offer.

## So there was no doubt Carol was dying.

She was dying in a few days. We all know that someday we will die. Not now, but in the future. Someday. We can put it out of our thinking. For most of us, we don't want to think about dying and really come to grips with what happens next, so we tuck such thoughts in the back of our minds. It is a form of passive denial. We will deal with it, but later.

In Carol's case, the thought of dying, the reality that she only had a few days to live, made dying the only focus that mattered. None of life's pursuits mattered anymore.

In stages, it dawned on me that she would never again go upstairs to her sewing room, never stitch another stitch, never cook a meal, never get dressed again, never compose at her computer, never even get out of bed again.

## Knowing that you are dying, not down the road, but in only days, forces a person to think about what happens after death. Every person must face it sooner or later.

If we rely on living a good life and being a good person as the safe passage into eternity, we could be nervous in our last days. Just how good is good enough?

## As for Carol, she knew she had not lived a perfect life.

She had some struggles and some failures. There had been harsh words, judgmental attitudes, traces of bitterness, and highly opinionated views. She knew how to argue her point!

Her lovely qualities of compassion, love of family, the sacrifice of time and energy, love of God, selflessness, and help for the needy, were obvious to all around her.

She knew she was dying in just a few days, knew she had not lived a perfect life, and yet she had no anxiety, no fear, no despondency, as her last days played out.

**My only explanation for her total lack of anxiety is she was not relying on her life being good enough to be welcomed into eternal life.**

She knew her failures, in spiritual terms, were called sin. Since God is Holy, no sin bearers are allowed in His presence. The impasse is resolved by the Son of God, Jesus, dying on the cross and His shed blood covering the sin of all who believe in Him. Sin is forgiven, thus one is made acceptable to Holy God.

**Carol, in her youth, embraced the truth that Jesus was the Son of God and that His shed blood was sufficient enough to cover all sin.**

She knew she was forgiven. She had total confidence she was Heaven bound, that Jesus knew her by name, that He had prepared a home for her, and that the hereafter was going to be pain-free in every way.

That life-changing reality was put to the test with the news of "days or weeks." Unshaken by death, she had composure and confidence and joy!

Her attitude was, "Escort Angels, Take Me Away!"

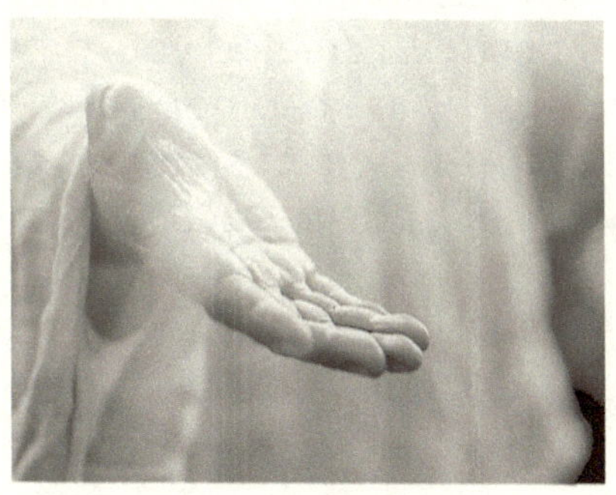

# Chapter 2: Six Weeks With Jesus

*Settling into glory.*

## Carol has been with Jesus for six weeks.

She is not a newbie anymore. Has she embroidered a glorious design in magnificent colors on the back of someone's robe? Has she been inducted into the "Artisans of Glory" cadre to embark on the next project to beautify the already supremely stunning banners of heaven?

## Has she stood, knelt, and prostrated before the throne to bask in the radiant glory no mortal could endure?

## What has the Savior had to say to her?

"I gifted you and you used it! Marvelous job my beloved! Many were touched, many challenged, many blessed, many loved. You were real as you reflected my compassion to those around you. You did exceedingly well."

## "Welcome to your new home...

...others should follow your lead in laying up treasures in

heaven, where no recession, no moth, no thief, no market crash, no fire can destroy. I created you, gifted you, enabled you, and you did exactly as I had hoped - - you acted on what I gave you to the benefit of so many. In doing so you have brought great joy and satisfaction to me, the I AM."

**It can rightly be said, "And Carol found favor in the eyes of the Lord."**

# **Chapter 3: Carol's Abode**

*What would a perfect dwelling be like for Carol?*

## "I go to prepare a place for you"

That's what Jesus said. What would a perfect dwelling be like for Carol? A place thought out, designed, carefully constructed, to more than please his faithful daughter?

## For starters, it would have color.

The color combination of Earth hues would be laced together in breathtaking sequences, causing one to audibly gasp in wonder. Mingled in the composition, the hints and splashes of New Order colors have a spellbinding effect on all who behold the wonder.

And the marvel for Carol is the full spectrum of Earth color and New Order color at her disposal, to create paintings of exquisite quality, to adorn any available blank space.

## The furniture would be soft to the touch...

...blended tones to please the eye, and inviting in contour,

as if to lovingly embrace any slightly weary soul.
The lightest touch would move any piece effortlessly to
a new location. Pure delight for one such as Carol. And a
marvel of the new domain is the lack of any lint or stray
popcorn remaining after any move. Any new arrangement
would result in perfect alignment for pleasant conversation.

## Outside her dwelling there would be flowers.

Blooming flowers of a vast array of color, size, and exhil-
arating fragrance. The paths and borders would weave
through rippling water ways and dancing fountains. Quaint
footbridges would be arched over waterways, filled with
lily pads and edged in cattails. Dragonflies of iridescent
greens and blues and purples make all the surroundings
quiver with color.

There would be hanging flower baskets, hosting a dense
array of blossoms, dazzling in color and contrast, with
trailing runners reaching the retaining walls, terracing the
slopes at hand. Those terraces radiate in all directions,
the refractions from the emerald, ruby, topaz, and jasper
adorning the garden.

## The Creator would have a Carol-specific studio for her.

Studio, in our minds, may conjure up a limited or small
space. Not so! It is large enough to house every supply
needed to inspire unlimited creativity. And it is open-ended
for expansion. New horizons, of yet untried expressions of
creativity, lurk in eternity.

Carol's fingers were seldom fiber free on Earth, so it is no
surprise to see the stunning array of thread and yarn and
fabric beckoning to her. Some items defy accurate description. How can it be? Gold and silver, spun as thin and soft
as silk. Fibers that catch the light like precious stones.

Fibers that flash color like a mallard duck, when tilted, are transparent.

Some fibers, when touched, ring forth a sweet note. The intensity of touch creates a melody of rising and falling notes. Those fibers, woven together, when touched or stroked, sound forth a symphony worthy of silence from all.

**Fiber, clay, paint, and pen can morph together into realms of beauty beyond Earth experience. All this brings joy upon joy. Unleashing a creative enthrallment which is pure praise to the Prince of Heaven.**

**The kitchen is not cluttered, but whatever utensil or pot she needs is there.**

The same for cooking supplies. No shopping or making do, when a supply is missing, it is there. The cooking heat is just right, so no more burned cheese sandwiches!

**A music parlor hosts the familiar piano for her to play and sing and exalt the Lord.**

Back a bit, as if in reserve, are unfamiliar instruments that are enticing to an adventurous soul such as Carol. She is sure to pick them up when the time is right.

## A veranda...

...a lovely place to sit, to take in the richness of the ponds and fountains and raised gardens, wraps around one corner.

*When He said, "I go to prepare a place for you," He vastly understated the beauty, the grandeur, the sheer loveliness, made just for his beloved Carol!*

## Welcome to your new abode!

# Chapter 4: New Arrivals

*Look forward to the thrilling day when you are
a new arrival in heaven.*

On a summer day, an accident in Prineville took the life of a jockey in his very first race. It seems tragic. I shake my head in disbelief, even though I did not know the man at all! What a reminder of how fragile life can be.

## This put my mind to thinking about heaven and the new arrivals there.

## Just how many new arrivals are there likely to be each day?

I found from Siri that, on average worldwide, 155,000 die each day. It is estimated that about 30% of the population is Christian. So, 30% of the deaths must be Christian, which totals 46,500.

The Guttmacher Institute calculates worldwide there are 200,000 abortions daily. All aborted babies, from every nation, every religion, every ethnic group, are Heaven-bound. They had no choice in their existence or destination. They are God's precious creation, destined for eternity with Him.

By combining the number of Christian deaths with the deaths of the unborn, we have a sum of about two hundred and fifty thousand deaths. Which means there are that many new arrivals in heaven daily. A quarter million daily. What a large group! I had no idea the number could be that large.

## So, "new arrivals" has to be a major department in heaven.

I know that nothing is overwhelming or taxing to God the almighty. But humanly speaking, the logistics of this would be daunting!

Let's start with the host of escort angels needed to transfer each earthling to their new abode in heaven. The account of the rich man and Lazarus dying bears witness that Lazarus was carried by angels to Abraham's side.

Lazarus was not alone. In fact, there were angels, plural. From this, I gather there had to be at least two. So assuming two angels escort each new arrival each day, a corps of 500,000 escort angels are needed.

Two angels, bringing one newbie, is a massive gathering of 750,000. Each day it is like that! That is equivalent to the population of Seattle at the "arrival center" of heaven every day.

I really don't have direct Biblical references for these ideas. But in my mind, in my reasoning, my own logical processing of the new arrivals scenario, is an attempt to grasp what it might be like. Bear with me.

## The largest group, by far, is the two hundred thousand unborn.

Their experience is unique. They have never seen any earthly thing. No land, no tree, no bird, no color, no parent, no mountains or streams. So the grandeur, the glory, the beauty, the sheer loveliness of heaven will be normal to them. It is all they will ever know.

The muted voices and music, as if heard underwater, are now distinct and clear. Not a sound is now missing. Sweet notes of praise resound and voices exalt the King Supreme! Without effort they know the universal language of their new domain. Fluent conversations, with full vocabulary, are theirs upon arrival.

The pain and anguish of their demise is now soothed completely. Now joy and comfort and bliss are the overwhelming sensation. Oh the touch of the Savior's healing hand! There is much to know and many to meet as they embark on their new eternal life, fully-formed.

**Just to aid my thinking, I have grouped the new arrivals into several more categories.**

**The next group are the "Barely Beginners."**

They heard the message, they believed, they became children of God. But before they heard, learned, or understood very much, their earthly life ended. So the new life in heaven is a thrilling experience! So many wonders of beauty and knowledge unfold daily, as they are continuously in a state of awe.

For the first time, hearing about Moses, the baby in the Nile, Abraham the new father of Isaac, David, taking on Goliath, Jesus, telling Peter he would make him a fisher of men. There is no rush. There is lots of time to get the full story and be able to take in the full glory of God.

## My next imagined category of new arrivals are the "Committed and Growing."

They are convinced they are on the right track and are seriously being transformed by the Holy Spirit living within them. God is real. The blood of Jesus really does cover all sin, being forgiven brings liberating, life-giving freedom, and the end result is absolutely no fear of death. These have known with confidence, that when their earth life was over, a new life awaited them. They look forward to spending eternity with the Creator of the universe--our heavenly father, Jesus the son--our redeemer, and the great crowd of believers from past ages, together with legions of mighty angels.

They knew, in some measure, what to expect but the impact of the glory of God, the encompassing triumphant praise, the overwhelming beauty, sends their senses reeling. They knew heaven would be great, but in reality it defied true description. Earth had its problems, but this new realm is peace and joy and pure loveliness. An immense treasure that all should aspire to.

## My next category is "Hall of Famers."

There are a few men and women in each generation that have a huge impact in their service to the Lord. It could come from their circumstance. Bart grew up with a very abusive father making his life miserable, but from it he composed "I can only imagine". The song touched hearts nationwide.

William Tyndale had linguistic skills. He translated the Bible into English, so ordinary people could read the Bible themselves. It changed lives, it changed nations!

Noah found favor in the eyes of the Lord. Through Noah, the world was saved during the great flood. Ordinary people in many ways, but amazing in other ways. I could be wrong, but I think their arrival into heaven was occasion for special attention. Their "Well done" must have resounded loud and clear!

## Every unborn, every young child, every born again Christian will be a new arrival someday.

What a day that will be! The wonder of seeing Jesus, being welcomed by Him by name. The joy of arrival, the reuniting with our beloveds, the beauty beyond compare, resettled in our new home, made just for us, is just the beginning. As days pass, the realities of our new home will be revealed to our limited understanding. Wonder upon wonder!

## Having been a builder in the past, I thought of all these new arrivals needing housing.

Jesus promised he would have a place ready when we arrive. Thinking about that, I just can't get my mind wrapped around it. There needs to be 250,000 new units ready everyday. In earthly terms, a 100 lot subdivision is a big project. It takes months of work, with machines working everyday, and workers galore. From surveyors to the asphalt pavers.

Once a lot is ready the houses start going up. Months and months of building, even years. That is for just 100 houses. So think of needing 250,000 every day!

Mistakenly, we may view Heaven as boring. Think again! New arrival center, processing, names recorded, new clothing, shuttle to their new address, introductions, tours, getting everyone resettled, questions answered.

## Heaven is a dynamic place where peace, joy, and love abound. You can look forward to the thrilling day you are a new arrival.

# Chapter 5: 16 Months in Heaven

*Imagine the breathtaking flurry of activity
Carol has experienced in heaven!*

**Yesterday was a minor anniversary. Sixteen months have passed and it set my mind to wondering just what my Carol is doing.**

An earlier calculation gave me an estimate of the number entering Heaven each day – about fifty thousand Christians and two hundred thousand unborn, terminated in the womb. Combined, this gives the sum of 250,000 daily new arrivals at the Gates of Glory. Daily!

Some simple math shocked me. These 16 months have been a breathtaking flurry of activity for Carol to behold. Since her arrival, 120 million have been welcomed into heaven. I can hardly grasp what it looks like. A hundred and twenty million in 16 months! That is a third of the population of the United States.

**There is some evidence that the Triune God is using those in his eternal domain to carry out his purposes.**

Angel Gabriel was sent to talk with Mary and Joseph. Michael did battle with the Prince of Persia. Angels were sent to protect Lot and an angel set Peter free from prison. So it is evident that God has assignments for His Holy Angels.

As for the Saints, there is some reason to believe they will also be given assignments. When Jesus returns at the last battle, the Saints return with Him and the new Heaven and new earth will be established.

If the parable of the minas given to the slaves of a nobleman is applied to heaven, it gives insight for our time in heaven. When the slaves gave account of their stewardship of the minas they had been given, the one who turned his one mina into ten was praised and told he would be given authority over ten cities. This suggests that those in heaven could be given responsibilities in the New Order.

The twenty-four elders worship and cast their crowns before the throne. They are actively engaged in the flow of Kingdom Life.

Abraham received the poor beggar named Lazarus when he died. As they were together, they addressed the rich man who also died and found himself in great agony, separated by a great chasm, so he could not come to them. There was dialogue and conversation. Abraham was on assignment.

And on earth, God chose to work through man to achieve his goals. Adam named the animals. Noah built the ark. The prophets spoke for God. His pattern on earth gives precedence for His likely mode of operation in heaven.

It is clear that God sends angels on assignments, there are many instances. There is limited evidence that God uses the residents of heaven to do his bidding and carry out Kingdom assignments.

## It is with these limited examples that I return to the hundred and twenty million new arrivals Carol has witnessed during her brief stay in heaven.

Assuming they, Father, Son, and Holy Spirit, don't just go "poof," and make everything happen like magic, but instead assign the host of new-order-citizens assignments to get all the kingdom activities done in perfect order. So, assuming the citizens are "employed" to make Kingdom life unfold in an orderly, seamless, welcoming, and glorious manner, is uncharted territory for me to contemplate.

When the citizens used to live on earth, they were gifted by God with talents, abilities, and perceptions, making each one a unique individual. So, each citizen is amazed to find they are asked to do what they are best able to do and what they love doing. God's enabling, put to full use, bringing Joy—absolute Joy, with each project.

## Carol's final great passion on earth was her embroidery machine stocked with drawers of thread of eye-popping colors.

This is a perfect match for citizen Carol. Each new arrival needs a new robe. They brought nothing with them. There is an immediate need for their robe. And the new robe must need a logo of something. A dove? Initials? A new name? Raised hands in praise?

I envision Carol's squadron of like-minded embroiderers gathered in her workshop parlor. Hundreds of them.

There, gold filament thread glistens, never tangles, ever flashing in the total light from every direction. Lightning-fast needle completing each task in seconds. The chatter is a hum of harmony and delight. The host of support workers can barely keep up, supplying fresh robes and quickly taking the completed ones to the new arrival center.

When God gifted each earthling, more than one talent was evident. There were variations in combinations. In Carol's case, the broad gifting was creativity. It manifested in many ways. Yes, the embroidery was pure delight!

## Then there was painting.

She tole painted, oil painted, acrylic, watercolor, colored pencils, pastel chalk, and watercolor pencils. She painted mountains, trees, flowers, faces, and yard art poles. Remember, 250,000 new housing units are needed – every day! If just one painting adorned each new dwelling, just think of the massive room, filled with easels and paint tubes and brushes of every size it would take. Artists from every culture would be pressed into service to bring forth stunning beauty on large canvas and small.

When their brush finds the burnt umber and Prussian Blue, touching the canvas seems to cause the color to flow in precise harmony with the whole composition. The colors, the blending, the brushstrokes, all combine to make gallery quality art. And the gallery is each new dwelling, ready to be occupied. Captivating splendor, sheer beauty!

I can almost see Carol's choice. Large canvas with orange poppies. Two are in full bloom, in all their splendor. A third has one petal missing and another is drooping. Behind are two with only the black pods remaining. The big splashes of color command a viewer's attention. You may look away but then you can't resist another look. You are drawn in, you can't look enough.

Some days are filled with needle and thread adorning logos on robes as soft as alpaca. Other days, the crimson red and burnt sienna beckons. Your scheduler changes up your area of service to keep interest high and creative juices flowing.

## There is an intensity of activity with brush and needle, but often, spontaneous praise breaks forth and spreads from group to group.

Notes of the sweetest adoration, traveling like tripped Domino's across the far reaches of the Kingdom, fading out of earshot even when straining to hear. One might hear the voices of a thousand, ten thousand perhaps, but over 100,000, the all-consuming chorus of voices fades to silence across the distance. A shout of joy erupts and then all hands resume the task before them.

When first experiencing the praise erupting all around, it so captivates and overwhelms a new citizen, they may just stand in awe, unable to join in. But it soon becomes evident that this praise, that gathers you up and totally engulfs you, as tremendous as it is, is normal in the Kingdom culture.

## Every time the wave of praise sweeps across the place, hearts are renewed. The joy and appreciation and love of Jesus the Savior, so fills each person, the praise just pours out.

## There's a huge contingent of new arrivals that are the transformed unborn.

Although they appear the same as all the other citizens, and have very adequate language skills, they have almost no knowledge of anything. Their redemption was secured by the "Writ of Unborn Protection" clause, recorded in antiquity.

They are highly beloved by the Prince and are enrolled in a tailor-made welcome course to acquaint and equip them for eternal life. It is true that the sin nature was DNA deep, but there was never a chance to actively sin. The Savior's blood cleansed them before they could act. They entered directly from the womb to heaven. The Savior knew and gifted them before they could live it.

So now, the accelerated learning begins. Their teachers and mentors come from the ranks of the seasoned followers of the Savior, Jesus.

## It is easy for me to picture citizen Carol eager to volunteer for such a duty.

There is history all need to grasp. Adam and Eve, Noah, Abraham, Moses, Jacob are just some of the highlights. The prophets and kings, their lives and exploits, must be laid out in full. And then the mystery of Jesus's transition from Heavenly Prince to earth baby, to master teacher, and then mankind Redeemer, needs revealing. So much to grasp. But the thrill of knowing the perfect culture to which they belong cements their contentment.

She would never tire of retelling each story, each event, and the personal touch of her own encounter and journey of earth life, led by the Spirit within.

The first fifty thousand she takes through the course, keeps her on her toes. But by the time she is taken 500,000 through the orientation, her confidence is solid. She has it down.

With a steady throng of new arrivals every day, the need for more mentors is evident. Her experience moves her up a notch, as a mentor-trainer and group overseer.

**There is never a dull moment, but somehow it is not rushed or stressful. The flow of life is orderly and actually serene. It is interesting and purposeful and joyful. Everyone is working at their assigned tasks with harmony and cooperation. No dissension erupts anywhere.**

The vast number inhabiting Heaven and how it all functions is beyond my ability to grasp. By my very basic calculations, there are billions of the redeemed already there. And Carol has been integrated into the kingdom culture, to her great delight. She has a place, a perfect place, to express her Godly gifting, to express her love of Jesus, to know and enjoy the flow of Heaven life, to have endless fellowship with so many she has loved.

## All of that in just 16 months.

It is hard to fathom what all she'll be able to encounter in 100 years or 5,000. There's music to play, gardens to groom, interviews with Noah and others she is eager to meet. Seeing creation displayed and so many fibers to manipulate. The list can go on and on. Seeing the sea like glass, the throne of God, the marvel and splendor of the New Jerusalem. So, my wondering what Carol might be doing, is undoubtedly beyond my wildest imaginations. She is fully engaged, I'm sure. And one day I'll experience firsthand all the wonders of Heaven for myself, when I too am a new arrival.

# Chapter 6: Heaven Has a Cure

*Whatever our trauma, hurt, disappointment, or failure, Heaven certainly has a cure.*

What we do know about heaven comes from bits and pieces that we fit together. Not a complete picture, but perceptions. The lion laying down with the lamb is one mental image we build upon.

The lion is known to us as the king of the jungle. He chases down and eats all sorts of critters in the area he roams. A lamb isn't big, strong, or fast. Easy prey. Tasty lunch.

So to picture just the opposite sends a message that Heaven must be tranquil indeed. The lamb has no worries, no anxiety over anything, and is not fussed up whatsoever.

**Attempting to apply this perception to dear Carol, having roamed heaven for months, is my earthbound challenge. Picture in my mind her struggles being over.**

## As best as I can recall her struggle with weight started after giving birth to our two sons.

In those early married days, her weight was a mild issue. She wished to be thinner and she worked at it with exercise and by watching what she ate.

For at least the last 35 years of her life, she was very frustrated with weight loss, only to gain it back. The many books on the shelf give witness that she read and researched every plan that came along.

And she was not one to take on a program half-heartedly. She would stick with it. In the midst of it, she would crave to eat what she wanted to eat. She was tired of sticking to a plan, especially when the weight loss was painfully slow.

She had lost 38 pounds just prior to the devastating chemo. The doctor told her some chemo patients lost weight taking the harsh chemo cocktail. Not Carol. The misery of the treatment was compounded by her steady gain.

Her hair all fell out, so she felt ugly as a monster: fat, ugly, and stripped of all energy – physical and emotional. For weeks on end there were tears. Lots of tears. Real anguish.

Even after surgery and a year-and-a-half recovery, the weight remained. She hated the mirror.

But then she was changed, in the "twinkling of an eye", as she was escorted by Holy Angels to her new Eternal home. I picture her new heavenly body as trim, fit, actually Eve-like. Never again to be tormented with unwanted weight. For Carol, her new body would be "Heavenly!"

## The second area of struggle, that I think her arrival in heaven cured, was her low self-esteem.

She recounted her childhood, and no matter how well she did in school, or band, or sewing, her father never said "Well done," but instead, "You can do better." This seemed to have imprinted her life with a compulsion to accomplish more.

If she was not busy producing a project of some sort, she felt unworthy. To everyone around her it was evident she was super accomplished in a wide variety of skills. To name a few, she painted, did stained glass, machine knitted, sewed everything, cooked, wrote twenty books, taught workshops, had a weekly radio program in Uganda, beaded, and rubber-stamped. I could go on, you get the drift. And she was good at all of it.

In the last weeks of her life I heard her confess a new revelation: she did not have to keep producing to be a worthy person. She was worthy by belonging to Jesus. She did not need to prove herself any longer. How I wish the realization had come when she was a young girl.

I picture her now, very content with herself, but still as creative as ever. Creativity is flowing out of her, fulfilling God's design. No longer driven, but set loose with an energized passion for color and design.

## The third area Carol struggled with was being liked.

She did not have many friends. In reality, many people held her in high regard, but she often felt alienated.

There was some truth to her alienation. It was linked to her spiritual gifting. She was a prophet, according to some scriptural gifts lists. This gave her a worldview that was right or wrong, with very little room for any middle ground. Issues were black or white.

And she seldom held back sharing her views. She was bold, vocal, and opinionated. She didn't mind being confrontational, and in her mind, she was almost always right. Compromise seldom suited her.

This is why she felt friendless and isolated much of the time.

The positive side of this gifting was that she was focused and got a lot done. She pushed through difficulties and got results. She could spot a lie or deception with uncanny accuracy.

Jesus said he was the Truth, the Way, and the Life. In heaven truth is absolute, so Carol will be in her element, proclaiming with boldness the truths of holiness, righteousness, purity, and fidelity. Her boldness, tenacity, and unwavering resolve will be a virtue, thoroughly admired. Her status in heaven will be exalted as an outstanding citizen of the domain.

**I visualize her now as a complete and fulfilled, even robust, participant of the New Order. Her heavenly body has no defect or imperfection. She is fully worthy in the eyes of the Lord and in all of heaven, and she is held in high esteem for her forthrightness and candor. She is beaming with approval, and purpose— engaged to the fullest!**

If the lamb can snug up to the lion for a noontime nap, the stage is set for ultimate tranquility. Whatever our trauma, hurt, disappointment, or failure, Heaven certainly has a cure. The God of Heaven is the cure!

31

* 9 7 9 8 2 1 8 4 9 0 2 0 1 *